P9-EKJ-884

Woodard, Bellen,
More than peach : changing
the world ... one crayon at a
[2022]
33305250166737
ca   07/28/22

N WOODARD
MORE than PEACH

"CHANGING THE WORLD...
ONE CRAYON AT A TIME!"

ILLUSTRATED BY FANNY LIEM

SCHOLASTIC INC.

To my parents & educators,
Thank you for safe spaces that cherish our curiosity and our humanity.
And thanks to you, the reader, for being you. BRILLIANT.
♥Bellen

© 2022 More than Peach, LLC. All rights reserved.
More than Peach, More than Peach Project, Crayon Activist, and Bellen are
protected trademarks of More than Peach, LLC.

All rights reserved. Published by Scholastic Inc., *Publishers* since 1920. SCHOLASTIC and associated
logos are trademarks and/or registered trademarks of Scholastic Inc.

The publisher does not have any control over and does not assume any responsibility for
author or third-party websites or their content.

No part of this publication may be reproduced, stored in a retrieval system, or transmitted in any form or by
any means, electronic, mechanical, photocopying, recording, or otherwise, without written permission of the
publisher. For information regarding permission, write to Scholastic Inc., Attention: Permissions Department,
557 Broadway, New York, NY 10012.

ISBN 978-1-338-80927-5

10 9 8 7 6 5 4 3 2 1   22 23 24 25 26
Printed in China   62

First printing 2022

All photos provided by the Woodard Family

Written by Bellen Woodard
Illustrated by Fanny Liem
Book design by Salena Mahina

HI!

I'm Bellen, president of Bellen's More than Peach Project™ and World's 1st Crayon Activist™—and now I can even add industry transformer! I began More than Peach after doing something I hadn't known I would ever do—and then creating products that ended up making a really big change.

My goal? To make sure that absolutely no kid feels "disincluded" in their spaces for simply being the human they're intended to be.

"More than Peach is about more than crayons."

My book will show you how I managed to transform my classroom (and more!) to make it supercool for everyone there AND how you can step in no matter how old you are to help lead the way—even when you think you could never do that. If you have questions or ideas after reading, you can even connect with me.

Can't wait to see what you do next:

I'M ROOTING FOR YOU!

—BELLEN WOODARD

"Rise and shine, Sunshine," is my wake-up call. But just for a moment, my eyes cling to last night's dreams, not yet ready to leave them behind.

My mornings are filled with smiles and a bump here and there.

We rush in the busyness the morning brings.

Being with my brothers is sort of like gazing into a mirror—their faces reflect mine.

Shades of the world with the same warm and curious eyes.

I sigh when I wave goodbye.
My brothers' reflections disappear
and leave only me.

But just one "me" is more than enough.
And I make so much of it!

Sometimes we might trip up, but we have friends to catch us.

School is a home away from home.

And when at home, we learn to grow.
"Does anyone have the skin-color crayon?" my friend asks.

Some call it the skin-color crayon. I've heard it many times before.

But this time when I pass the peach-colored crayon to him, something in me feels different.

"Can someone pass me the skin-color crayon?" another friend asks later.
The question rings through the room.

This question didn't seem to bother my teachers. Or my friends.

Why was I the only one feeling confused?

My mom and I celebrate the day. We share lots of stories and giggles.

I also tell her about "the skin color" crayon language. I explain that even though the question puzzles me, I always pass the peach crayon.

"Well, our skin color is brown. So next time, why not just hand over the brown crayon instead?" Mom says.

But that doesn't
feel right, either.

I think for a while,
and the idea hits me!

"No, Mom. Instead, I'll ask what color they want," I answer. "Because it can be any *number* of beautiful colors."

And so, the next time that question rings out, I reply:

"Which one? Skin can be any number of beautiful colors."

"Oh yeah! I meant the peach color," my friend says.

Suddenly, I realize that if this friend could understand, maybe my other friends could, too.

Again and again, I get asked the same question.

Again and again, I reply the same way.

Gently, knowingly, trying to change the language.

Until I finally hear an echo. My teacher replies just the way I did.

"Of course!" she says.
"What crayon color would
you like? Because skin tones
can be any number of
beautiful colors."

I had been the spark, and now my whole classroom is lit up.

It's so important that your space is brilliant. Just like you.

Soon the new language rippled through the school. If I can make such a big change here, I can also make it happen at other schools!

I put my idea to paper,
and my family helps me plan.

Growing isn't always easy.
Change is a team effort.

And the bigger your team, the faster change happens!

I lead the way and ask my friends, school, and whole community for help.

All around the world, the language is changing. Minds are growing.

And we will keep going until the world knows we're more—much more—than peach. We're each!

Together we can show the world the power of kidhood —one crayon at a time!

SCHOOL SHOP

"INSTEAD OF ASKING KIDS WHAT THEY WANT *to be* WHEN THEY GROW UP, ASK THEM WHAT THEY WANT *to change.*"

♥ Bellen

BELLEN WOODARD is president of Bellen's More than Peach Project™, the World's 1st Crayon Activist™, and the pioneer of "skin-color" crayons, and now an industry transformer! As the first of its kind, Bellen's innovative and inclusive art brand and project have become an international movement centering on empathy and youth leadership.

In spring 2019, at just eight years old, Bellen launched More than Peach with the primary goal of growing conversations and access: "getting multicultural crayons in the hands of all students" to increase empathy, creativity, and leadership so absolutely no kid is "disincluded." This came after having forever changed the "skin-color" crayon language in her own classroom and school! She has since enacted wide-scale change around the world.

Bellen's growing impact now felt across cultures and generations—inducing even the largest art brands and others to follow—and she is a face of a new generation of product inclusion. She began her mission—with her principal's endearing support—by hosting a drive at her school. Her ingenuity and compassion inspired students in all grades to join in, including spearheading their own community drives, helpful initiatives, and solutions! Her principal shared that he had never seen anything quite like it!

Bellen continues to make history, including having her crayons and art bundles, as well as her story, included in museum exhibits. She has also earned many top honors, including proclamations and her crayons and art bundles are now even in museums! Bellen has also been recognized in a cover story for Scholastic News, named TIME's Kid-of-the-Year Top Five, Anti-Defamation League Honoree, The Root Top 25 Futurist, and featured in *Vanity Fair* Italy, *NBC Nightly News with Lester Holt*, and many other top media outlets across the world. Her uniquely designed message and More than Peach art supplies are now available in Target stores to reach more students nationwide!

A voracious reader, Bellen began reading at age two and enjoys creative writing (and, secretly, loves school projects). She has also been a professional model since age six, and is a ballet and lyrical dancer, and author. She has met and recently published interviews with *TIME/TIME for Kids* with former First Lady Michelle Obama, Dr. Mae Jemison, and Secretary of Education Dr. Miguel Cardona. And, importantly, this Young Mensan is now a middle schooler and sixth grader! To learn more about More than Peach, connect with Bellen, or to order your very own products, visit morethanpeach.com.

HOW TO...
Grow Your Space

DID YOU KNOW THAT THE PEACH CRAYON WAS ACTUALLY NAMED "FLESH"?

I found it pretty strange that there was just one crayon with that name and that even today only one was being called "the skin-color" crayon. So with More than Peach, I wanted every single person to know I value them and that their spaces (and businesses) really should, too! So my answer was to create "skin-colored" crayons that are all actually named, what else but, "skin color." This was to help us find a true narrative that would consider everyone—and so my crayons can have a conversation with every kid using them so that they can see representations of not only themselves, but of others.

WHAT DO YOU WANT TO GROW?

Is it space exploration, kindness, conservation, or maybe an invention, like one to keep your jewelry from getting tangled? I mean, who knows? Would you like to see a change in your school or maybe at home? Well, what are you waiting for?!

It starts by leading with L.O.V.E., which just means:

LIFT OUR VOICES EVERYWHERE

LIFT

First, dream big and see the possibilities. Believe in you and what you're doing because you're gonna be the one to make your idea(s) soar. And believe in those around you, too.

OUR VOICES

Next, be ready to talk about it. You can even call this a pitch but really it's sharing your idea to help others understand. If they don't end up understanding, don't worry because everyone may not. But if it's important to you, keep going. Or as Dr. Mae Jemison once told me, "Don't shrink!"

Support is great! Maybe when you start out, you're the only one. But if it's about growing a space and not making it smaller, remember to consider others, too. It's okay if you're not the loudest or that you don't talk about it all the time, but be sure to let others know how you feel and why this is important to you. Schedule a meeting with your principal or your parents OR even your *siblings*. Yes, *them*.

EVERYWHERE

Your message and your voice deserve to be in any space you're invested in. One thing I try to do is leave these kinds of spaces better than I found them. This may not be the easiest thing you've ever done but it's worth it. Remember, see the possibilities! That's important. How much does your mission actually matter to you?

HERE ARE SOME HELPFUL STEPS:

- Read about others like you who've made a difference! **Important tip:** Be sure to learn about those who remind you of you but also those who may look different or have different talents and abilities. How exciting is that?!

- Ask your librarian, teachers, or parents for help. Explain your goals (and don't forget to share with them the important tip above).

- If you have second thoughts or are nervous, talk about that, too. Because I bet you're not the only one.

HOW TO...
Start a Drive

A **drive** is just a way to bring everyone together to help others. It's how I started my bigger project. Sometimes, students may lead a coat drive for the winter or a toy drive for the holidays. In my case, I sponsored an arts supplies drive with the goal of building relationships with everyone in mind. **What type of drive would you like to start?**

I wasn't sure what to expect from my very first drive, but the most important thing was to get people moving! I definitely never knew that it would spread all over the world. And that one drive at my school had a huge ripple effect, and kids as young as kindergartners (maybe even preschoolers?) began their own!

HERE'S HOW YOU CAN, TOO:

1. START SMALL. Think about a challenge you see. What does making it better look like to you? How can you make it better?

2. TALK ABOUT IT WITH SOMEONE YOU TRUST. Getting feedback from others can be very helpful, but remember—this is your project so definitely trust yourself enough to come up with your own solution!

3. GATHER YOUR THOUGHTS. If you can, write a summary of the problem and how you want to address it. Or talk it through. You can even practice by making a few videos with friends. Let your positive passion shine because as we grow, it's important that our spaces do, too. What's your small and big goals? Map out when your drive starts and ends. What supplies will you need to start? How will you get those supplies? How will you get the word out?

4. REMEMBER: YOU MEAN BUSINESS. You can host a drive in your home or classroom. Or you could have the bigger goal to include your whole school (or community). Any one is fine but don't be afraid to start small.

5. BELIEVE IN THE POWER OF YOU AND "KIDHOOD!" You're about to make your space even better. And that matters!

6. MEET WITH YOUR PRINCIPAL OR PARENT. Remember your pitch? This is where it'll come in handy. If you want help, ask one or a few others who you think will be helpful partners to join you. Don't worry if you're nervous or don't feel as prepared as you'd like. Everyone's learning. But in your meeting, explain how you would like to make a difference. And be proud of the work you've done so far. Great job!

7. PREPARE FOR THE BIG DAY.

8. LAUNCH your kickoff and keep sharing! Your kickoff is a big day but that doesn't mean you have to have a huge one. "There's no coloring rule book, right?" So make the day special in your own way.

9. NOW JUST KEEP AT IT and adjust if or when you need to. Send out updates and reminders. Let others know what's still needed and remind your community how many days are left. This can be done through some of the same ways you introduced your drive.

Well, that's the gist of it. And you can follow me or visit my website for more details or to see what I'm up to. I would love to hear how it's going with you. Remember, your dreams are MORE and they start with you!

THINGS YOU CAN DO

GATHERING SUPPLIES:

If you can earn money to help your project, that's great! I started my project using money I'd saved from modeling. You can also reach out to your school's parent organization to help get started.

WAYS TO PUBLICIZE AND PROMOTE YOUR DRIVE AND GOALS:

Create flyers

Morning news

School newsletter

Posters

Promote through the school's parent organization